Short. Smart.
Seriously useful.

Free ebooks and reports from O'Reilly
at oreil.ly/ops-perf

Get even more insights from industry experts
and stay current with the latest developments in
web operations, DevOps, and web performance
with free ebooks and reports from O'Reilly.

Cloud Foundry
The Cloud-Native Platform

Duncan C. E. Winn

Beijing · Boston · Farnham · Sebastopol · Tokyo

Cloud Foundry

by Duncan C. E. Winn

Printed in the United States of America.

Published by O'Reilly Media, Inc., 1005 Gravenstein Highway North, Sebastopol, CA 95472.

O'Reilly books may be purchased for educational, business, or sales promotional use. Online editions are also available for most titles (*http://safaribooksonline.com*). For more information, contact our corporate/institutional sales department: 800-998-9938 or corporate@oreilly.com.

Editor: Brian Anderson	**Interior Designer:** David Futato
Production Editor: Nicole Shelby	**Cover Designer:** Ellie Volckhausen
Copyeditor: Amanda Kersey	

January 2016:   First Edition

Revision History for the First Edition
2016-01-25:   First Release

978-1-491-96578-8

[LSI]

To my wife, Tanya. Thank you for moving halfway around the world in pursuit of my dreams.

Table of Contents

Foreword

Continuous Innovation and the Cloud Foundry Phenomenon

We are living through a time of accelerating change. It is not just our imagination or our subjective biases that makes it feel this way. Not only do our basic materials for augmenting our intelligence and capabilities get cheaper and more powerful every year, but they are being applied in more ways this month than they were last month, this year than they were last year. The volume change is larger when it is measured by the number of people affected. In The Innovator's Way (*http://innovators-way.com/*), Robert Dunham and Peter Denning offer a definition of innovation: "the number of people who change their behavior in order to adopt a new technology or product."

Because we are in a period when the Internet is still expanding to connect all of humanity, the number of people who are changing their behavior is historically unprecedented. As of 2015, three billion people are connected to the Internet; by 2020, there will be seven billion. This is 10 times the population of the United States and 3 times the population of China coming online across the world in only 5 years. At the same time as these "new activations" take place, those who have been on the Internet for decades are also newly activating a range of new devices along with the PCs and smartphones they have come to rely on.[1]

These new devices are themselves only the tip of the iceberg. The Industrial Internet is already showing signs of growing faster than the established, human-centric Internet. Wind turbines, factory equipment, farm machines, jet engines, and a wild array of industrial equipment are starting to send data automatically to data centers that can analyze the information into meaningful results, improving yields, expediting maintenance, and reducing failures and fatalities.

---

1 By 2020, there will be at least 50 billion devices directly connected to the Internet.

It is small wonder that enterprises are having a hard time keeping up. Born in a time of relative stability and raised on the ideas of *sustainable competitive advantage*, the world's largest companies and greatest employers have established financial, business, and technical practices focused on cornering a market through cost, access, or customer control and then trying to extend that advantage forever. As an indicator of the pace of change and the failure of this "common sense" approach to strategy, we can observe that since 2000, 52% of the Fortune 500 are no longer on that list. This is a massive shift in a short amount of time relative to the history of business.

Rita Gunter McGrath, a professor at the Columbia Business School, has done quantitative and qualitative analysis of this shift. From her empirical research, she has offered a new frame of reference: that we are at the end of competitive advantage. Upending status quo, she notes that the companies that have thrived in this turbulent transition have demonstrated four key traits: continuous reconfiguration, options valuation, constructive disengagement, and innovation proficiency.

The first three of these are deep areas in themselves and represent changes in business culture and practice that lead to scientific and experiment-led discovery and development of businesses, including letting businesses go when their time of growth inevitably comes to an end. These topics can be best explained and implemented by experts in the fields of change management, finance, and business strategy.

The last area, innovation proficiency, is the one that those of us who have grown up in the melting pot—and occasionally furnace—of Silicon Valley have some experience with and therefore something to offer every major company on the planet. We have a model some call "innovate or die" in reference to the funding patterns and resulting company lifecycles for software startups. This model works well partly because bad ideas run out of money, freeing the people who built them to leave, learn, and try again, with significantly lower cost when compared to failures in a classic global enterprise. The other reason it works well is because our new businesses are built on technology platforms, and we have developed practices that allow us to build those businesses quickly and iterate them based on feedback from customers on weekly or daily cycles.

This flywheel of learning and practice has led to breakout successes that are redefining the global economy. It is time for every enterprise to benefit from the hard lessons we have learned. Faster cycles are enabled by smaller teams and faster tools. The systems we build need to be secure and reliable, and they need to let us apply today's insights into tomorrow's product. These software best practices—not the practices of prior decades—are the ones we want to give to the rapidly transforming world of business.

The engineers and thinkers behind Cloud Foundry have spent the last five years incorporating the best practices of Silicon Valley into an open source software code base that is accessible to all and free to use. Our collective goal is to save a massive amount of time, effort, and inefficiency for people worldwide who are trying to move their companies forward at the new speed of business. We have built an independent nonprofit, the Cloud Foundry Foundation, as the keeper of this *software commons* to ensure the primacy of user needs and the long-term dependability of the ecosystem of developers and technologies around Cloud Foundry.

The phenomenon that is Cloud Foundry continues to accelerate, gaining users, contributors, and evangelists at an ever-faster pace. With this runaway growth, we can now set our vision on becoming the global standard for application platforms. With a broadly deployed platform, we can create a new and efficient market for enterprise software applications, which has long been a fragmented and inefficient phenomenon.

We believe every company in the world is going through a digital transformation to match the demands of customers, partners, and employees. It is our hope that the software that we are building helps you succeed, and we invite you to join us as members of this movement and as authors of your own software-defined future.

—Sam Ramji, CEO, Cloud Foundry Foundation

August 19, 2015, San Francisco, California

CHAPTER 1

Introduction

"Nobody has ever built cloud-native apps without a platform. They either build one themselves or they use Cloud Foundry."

—Joshua McKenty, *Field CTO of Pivotal Cloud Foundry*

We live in a world where connecting information to actions via software is the lifeblood of business. To thrive in this world, you need the ability to deliver software quickly, repeatedly, and with regular feedback. Cloud-native platforms are a way of achieving this. However, companies with an established process, organization style, and culture often find it challenging to make the transition to cloud-native platforms.

This book looks at the changes required to become cloud native and explores how Cloud Foundry can help.

Cloud Foundry is a platform for running applications and services. Its purpose is to change the way applications and services are deployed and run by reducing the *develop to deployment* cycle time. Cloud Foundry directly leverages cloud-based resources so that applications running on the platform can be infrastructure unaware. It provides a contract to run cloud-native applications predictably and reliably.

The platform space is complex. Different offerings have divergent feature sets and value propositions. Comparisons between platform technologies can be difficult. This book aims to cut through the confusion by unpacking the current practices in developing and delivering software quickly and showing how cloud-native platforms are an essential piece of that story.

The Competitive Advantage

Historically, the traditional way to deliver business value was to identify your competitive advantage and set up a process to make that advantage sustainable. This model has been transformed through software.

Marc Andreessen famously wrote an article for the Wall Street Journal titled "Software is Eating the World" (*http://bit.ly/software_eating_world*). This phrase helped shape a generation that thinks differently about IT. It encapsulates an important concept: there will not be a market in the world that will not be disrupted in some way by software.

Over the past decade, there has been a *shifting state* of established market leaders from market dominance to—in some cases—extinction. Companies are now constantly challenged to compete at the pace of change of a startup, coupled with competing against the clout of "Internet scale." Regardless of who said it first, if you are not embracing technology to deliver value to your customers, then you are losing out to someone who is.

However, to disrupt a market, it is not enough to have software at your core. Many companies have some level of software at their core, but not all are disrupting their industry. What distinguishes market-disrupting companies is the way they deliver software. Companies such as Netflix, Uber, and Airbnb are frequently commended for their use of technology. Increasingly, however, longer established companies such as Philips, GE, Allstate, and Mercedes are changing their software development and delivery model to not only remain competitive, but to embark on new and innovative commercial offerings.

Market-disrupting companies differ from incumbents because they can repeatedly deliver software, with velocity, through iterative development cycles of short duration.

The Development-Feedback Cycle

Any development cycle must include a constant feedback loop from end users for continually refining your product.

This constant *development-feedback* cycle enables companies to react to shifting demand and focus attention on the key areas receiving the most customer traction. It has allowed companies to redefine and then refine new business models and markets that consumers have been enthusiastic to embrace.

Companies with an established development-feedback cycle often provide services that are a joy to use, offering ways of interaction that were previously unavailable. If an unsatisfactory release is shipped, it can be updated quickly in the minimum amount of time, often measured in minutes or hours. For example, if I use Uber to book a taxi in the morning, the application may have been updated by the time I use it in the evening. In short, a constant development-feedback cycle allows you to try out new ideas, quickly identify failings, acknowledge feedback, rapidly adapt, and repeat.

Once you start delivering value to your customers, a constant development-feedback cycle then paves the way to maintaining value. You do not stop when you succeed. Ongoing iterative development allows for continuous adjustment to match and exceed consumer demands.

Velocity Over Speed

In every marketplace, speed wins. However, raw speed alone is insufficient. With speed alone, it is possible to run in circles or random directions and achieve very little. You need velocity.

Velocity, as a vector quantity, is direction aware. In our case, direction is based on feedback. Put another way, direction is dictated by what resonates with the customer. Speed must be coupled with the aforementioned constant development-feedback cycle to ensure progress in the right direction. As discussed, feedback is essential for continually refining your product so as to resonate with user expectations. Speed coupled with the development-feedback cycle produces velocity, and velocity is the only way to move both quickly and securely.

The Critical Challenge

Now, step back and think about what you need in order to ship software at velocity. Ask yourself if any of the following statements are true:

- You prefer to deploy software in hours or days, but you actually deploy in weeks or months.
- You have a single large code base.
- You cannot update one software component without impacting and redeploying everything else.
- Product innovation is stifled.
- Developers seem unmotivated or have low morale.
- The management team cannot figure out why software releases do not ship quickly.
- Your code is "buggy" with too much technical debt.[1]

If you currently identify with any of the previous statements, then the next question that needs addressing is: *"How can I solve problems?"* The reality is that these problems are solved by changing the current *process*, *organization*, and *culture*, in order to allow for fast and frequent deployments.

Many enterprises are aware of these current concerns. The enterprises that realize that process, organizational, and cultural changes are required to achieve a solution to these problems tend to quickly identify this as a critical challenge.

---

1 Technical debt refers to the eventual overhead of any software system. The debt can be thought of as the additional work required to deal with system constraints, prior to completing a particular job. For example, if an application has made extensive use of application-server-specific APIs, then technical debt occurs in removing those API calls when the application moves between application servers.

This challenge of addressing these three areas should not be underestimated. It is hard! For instance, consider provisioning new servers and middleware without a platform. Without preexisting resources and a self-service capability, handoffs occur between teams, which slow down the process. To change how servers are provisioned requires a change to the process, the organizational structure, and ultimately the delivery culture.

Cloud-native platforms provide a focal point that centers that change. They make it easier to do the right thing because everything you need to deliver software is already built into a platform. Without platform capability, you are required to slow right down as you adopt, integrate, and maintain more of the pieces of the technology stack.

Becoming Cloud Native

Cloud native is a term describing software designed to run and scale reliably and predictably on top of potentially unreliable cloud-based infrastructure.

Cloud-native applications are purposefully designed to be infrastructure unaware, meaning they are decoupled from infrastructure and free to move as required.

To not be cloud native means that applications need to be explicitly infrastructure aware, as they cannot reliably and predictably leverage cloud-based resources in a seamless manner. For example, consider running an application on a virtual machine (VM) in an IaaS environment. If your application is writing to the local file system, and the VM dies and gets recreated on a different storage device, then the application data is lost. In this scenario, the application is not cloud native because it is not leveraging the underlying cloud-based resources in a reliable way.

Becoming cloud native involves three fundamental tenets:

Automated Infrastructure Management and Orchestration
    This is the ability to consume infrastructure elastically (scale up and down), on demand, and in a self-service fashion. This layer is often referred to as Infrastructure as a Service (IaaS); however, it is the automated self-service characteristics of the infrastructure that are important. There is no explicit requirement to use virtualized infrastructure.

Platforms

You should use the highest level of abstraction possible to drive the underlying infrastructure and related services. Service abstraction is provided by a platform that sits above the infrastructure/IaaS layer, leveraging it directly. Platforms offer a rich set of services for managing the entire application life cycle.

The Twelve-Factor App

Ensure that the application layer on top of the platform can scale and thrive in a cloud environment. This is where the concept of The Twelve-Factor App (*http://12factor.net*) becomes key. Twelve Factor describes 12 design principles for applications purposefully designed to run in a cloud environment. These applications designed to run on top of a cloud-based infrastructure are typically referred to as cloud-native applications. Cloud-native applications are infrastructure unaware; they allow the platform to leverage infrastructure on their behalf. Being infrastructure agnostic is the only way applications can thrive in a cloud environment.[2]

By adopting these three tenets, everything you need to run and scale your applications—like your infrastructure, middleware services, user authentication, aggregated logging, and load-balancing—is already in place.

Becoming cloud native is an essential step in establishing a timely development-feedback cycle because it helps companies achieve velocity deploying software releases into production.

Undifferentiated Heavy Lifting

Most enterprises outside the information technology industry do not generate revenue from selling software; they leverage software to drive value into their core business. Non-IT companies have historically viewed IT as a cost center and have a hard time justifying the cost associated with developing and supporting software.

If you are spending significant time and effort building bespoke environments for shipping software, refocusing investment back

---

2 I like to recommend an ebook by Matt Stine on developing cloud-native applications: Migrating to Cloud-Native Application Architectures (*http://www.oreilly.com/program ming/free/migrating-cloud-native-application-architectures.csp*).

into your core business would provide a huge payoff. A good cloud-native platform allows enterprises to refocus effort back into the business by removing as much of the undifferentiated heavy lifting as possible. Examples of undifferentiated heavy lifting include:

- Provisioning VMs, middleware, and databases
- Creating and orchestrating containers
- User management
- Load balancing and traffic routing
- Centralized log aggregation
- Scaling
- Security auditing
- Providing fault tolerance and resilience

If you do not have a platform to abstract the underlying infrastructure and provide the above capabilities, this additional burden of responsibility remains yours.

Platforms Benefit Developers

Developers are no longer required to deal with middleware and infrastructure complexity. The platform leverages middleware and infrastructure directly, allowing streamlined development through self-service environments. This allows developers to focus on delivering applications that offer business value. Applications can then be bound to a wide set of available backing services that are available on demand.

Platforms Benefit Operations

The platform provides responsive IT operations, with full visibility and control over the application life cycle, provisioning, deployment, upgrades, and security patches. Several other operational benefits exist, such as built-in resilience, security, centralized user management, and better insights through capabilities such as aggregated metrics and logging.

Platforms Benefit the Business

The business no longer needs to be constrained by process or organizational silos. Cloud-native platforms provide a contractual promise to allow the business to move with velocity and establish the developer-feedback loop.

Chapter Summary

Technology is used to achieve a competitive advantage, but technology alone has never been enough. The world needs to fundamentally change the way it builds and deploys software in order to succeed in the hugely competitive markets that exist today. Cloud-native platforms provide the most compelling way to enable that fundamental shift.

CHAPTER 2

Adapt or Die

"There are two approaches to handling change: adapt or die vs. same mess for less!"

—Dekel Tankel, *Senior Director of Pivotal Cloud Foundry*

The first adage is true for all businesses: you either adapt and evolve to changes in the surrounding environment, or you die! As a company, you need to avoid becoming extinct. Aim to be Amazon, not Borders.

Businesses today are constantly pressured to adopt the myriad of technical driving forces impacting software development and delivery. These driving forces include:

- Anything as a service
- Cloud computing
- Containers
- Agile
- Automation
- DevOps
- Microservices
- Business-capability teams
- Cloud-native applications

This chapter explores each of these driving forces. The next chapter will explore how Cloud Foundry is uniquely positioned to leverage these forces.

Anything As A Service

In today's world, services have become the de facto standard. Today's premise is *anything as a service* (or XaaS). Services can be publicly hosted on the web or internal to a private data center. Every layer of information technology, from networking, storage, computation, and data, right through to applications, are all offered "as a service." We have now reached the point where if you are not leveraging compute resources as a service, it is unlikely that you are moving at the pace required to stay competitive.

The move to consuming services, beyond simply provisioning virtual machines (VMs) on demand, allows you to build your software against the highest level of abstraction possible. This approach is beneficial. You should not build everything yourself; you should not reinvent the wheel. To do so is costly, in terms of both time and money. It shifts focus and talent away from your revenue-generating business. If there is a service out there that has been deployed and managed in a repeatable and scalable way, becoming a consumer of that service allows you to focus on software supporting your revenue-generating business.

Cloud Computing

To understand the importance of today's cloud application platforms, it is important to understand the progression of platforms in IT. Cloud computing is the third incarnation of the *platform eras*:

- The first era was the mainframe, which dominated the industry from the 1950s through the early 1980s.
- Client-server architecture was established as the dominant second platform from the 1980s right up until the second decade of the 21st century.
- The "as a service" movement in IT has broadly been termed cloud computing, and it defines the third platform era we live in today.

With a move toward cheaper x86 based hardware, cloud computing allowed for *converged infrastructure*, moving away from dedicated infrastructure silos toward grouping commodity infrastructure components (e.g., servers, networks, and storage) into a single pool. This converged infrastructure provided better utilization and reuse of resources. As I discuss below, cloud computing has been subdivided into "as a service" layers (SaaS, PaaS, IaaS, etc). Regardless of the layer, there are three definitive attributes of "as a service":

Elasticity
> The ability to handle concurrent growth through dynamically scaling the service up and down at speed.

On demand
> The ability to choose when and how to consume the required service.

Self-service
> The ability to directly provision or obtain the required service without time-consuming ticketing.

These three tenets of XaaS describe the capability of provisioning cloud resources on demand as required. This self-service capability is a shift from procuring resources through a ticketing system involving handoffs and delays between developers and operations.

Platform as a Service

IaaS and SaaS are generally well understood concepts.

Software as a service (SaaS) is the layer at the top of the software stack closest to the end user. SaaS provides the ability to consume software services on demand without having to procure, license, and install binary packages.

The bottom layer of the "as a service" stack is known as infrastructure as a service (IaaS). This provides the ability to leverage cloud-based resources including networking, storage, compute (CPU), and memory. This is what most people think of when they hear the phrase *"moving to the cloud."* The IaaS layer includes both private clouds typically deployed inside a company's data center and public clouds hosted via the Internet.

A technology platform leverages underlying resources of some kind to provide a set of higher-level services. Users are not required to understand how the lower-level resources are leveraged because platforms provide an abstraction of those resources. Users only interact with the platform.

A cloud-native platform describes a platform designed to reliably and predictably run and scale on top of potentially unreliable cloud-based infrastructure.

Many companies leverage IaaS for delivering software, with developers requesting VMs on demand. IaaS adoption alone, however, is not enough. Developers may be able to request and start a VM in minutes, but the rest of the stack—the middleware service layers and application frameworks—are still required, along with setting up, securing, and maintaining multiple environments for things like QA, performance testing, and production. As a higher abstraction above IaaS and middleware, cloud-native platforms take care of these concerns for you, allowing developers to keep their focus on developing their business applications.

If you do not use a platform for running applications, you are required to orchestrate and maintain all the state-dependent information yourself. This approach sets a lower boundary for how fast things can be recovered in the event of a failure.

Platforms drive down the mean time to recovery because they leverage patterns that are predictable, automatable, and repeatable, with known and defined failure and scaling characteristics.

Containers

In recent years, there has been a rapid growth in container-based technologies (such as LXC, Docker, Garden, and Rocket). Containers offer three distinct advantages over traditional VMs:

1. Speed and efficiency
2. Greater resource consolidation
3. Application stack portability

Because containers can leverage a "slice" of a pre-built machine or VM, they are generally regarded to be much faster to create than a new VM. This also allows for a greater degree of resource consolidation, since many containers can be run in isolation on a single machine.[1] In addition, they have enabled a new era of application stack portability because applications and dependencies developed in a container can be easily moved and run in different environments.

Understanding Containers

Containers typically use primitives such as control groups, namespaces, and several other OS features to control resources and isolate and secure the relevant processes. Containers are best understood as having two elements:

- **Container images**: These package a repeatable runtime environment (encapsulating your application, dependencies, and file system) in a way that allows for images to be moved between hosts. Container images have instructions that specify how they should be run but they are not explicitly self-executable, meaning they cannot run without a container management solution.

- **A container management solution**: This often uses kernel features such as Linux namespaces to run a container image in isolation, often within a shared kernel space. Container management solutions arguably have two parts: the frontend management component known as a container engine such as Docker-engine or Garden-Linux, and the backend container runtime such as runC or runV.

---

1 The terms VM and machine and used interchangeably because containers can run in both environments.

Agile

Agile software development can best be understood by referring to the Agile Software Development Manifesto (*http://agilemani festo.org/*). Being agile means you are adhering to the values and practices defined in the agile manifesto. This manifesto values:

1. Individuals and interactions over processes and tools
2. Working software over comprehensive documentation
3. Customer collaboration over contract negotiation
4. Responding to change over following a plan

There are specific agile software development methods, such as *Extreme Programming (XP)*. XP values communication, simplicity, feedback, courage, and respect. Agile software development methods help teams respond to unpredictability through incremental, iterative work cadences (sometimes referred to as *sprints*). They focus on delivering smaller features more frequently as opposed to tackling one epic task at a time. The Agile methodology is an alternative to traditional sequential development strategies, such as the waterfall approach.

Many enterprises have moved toward embracing agile. Most teams now define epics that are broken down into smaller user stories weighted by a point system. Stories are implemented over sprints with inception planning meetings, daily standups, and retrospective meetings to showcase demonstrable functions to key stakeholders. Some companies have further adopted the agile disciplines of paired programming and test-driven development. However, the most critical piece of agile is often omitted: each iteration must finish with software that is able to be deployed into production. This allows for new features to be placed into the hands of real end users exactly when the product team decides, rather than only after reaching a significant milestone.

Agile can be a challenge for development teams who are not in a position to quickly deploy their applications with new features. Traditional release cycles of code, batched up and merged into a later release train, means that they forego regular end-user feedback. This feedback is the most valuable and most critical kind of feedback required. In essence, these teams adopt many of the agile principles without actually being agile. It is no use employing a "run, run, run" approach to development if you are subsequently unable to release software into production. Agile deployment allows teams to test out new ideas, quickly identify failings with rapid feedback, learn, and repeat. This approach promotes the willingness to try new things and ultimately should result in products more tightly aligned to end-user expectations.

Automate Everything

Operational practices around continuous integration (CI) and continuous delivery (CD) have been established to address the following two significant pain points with software deployment:

- Handoffs between different teams cause delays. Handoffs can occur during several points throughout an application life cycle, starting with procuring hardware, right through to scaling or updating applications running in production.
- Release friction describes the constant need for human interaction as opposed to using automation for releasing software.

Deployment pipelines are *release processes* automated by tooling to establish repeatable flows. They enable the integration and delivery of software to production. Deployment pipelines automate manual tasks and activities, especially around integration testing. Repeatable flows of code mean that every release candidate goes through the same set of integration steps, tests, and checks. This pipeline enables releases to production with minimal interaction (ideally just at the push of a button). When establishing deployment pipelines, it is important to understand the progression of continuous integration and continuous delivery.

Continuous Integration

Continuous integration (CI) is a development practice. Developers check code into a central *shared* repository. Each check-in is verified by automated build and testing, allowing for early detection problems and consistent software releases.

Continuous integration has enabled streamlined efficiencies for the *story to demo* part of the cycle. However, continuous integration without continuous delivery into production means you only have what Dave West has called water-Scrum-fall (*http://sdtimes.com/*

analyst-watch-water-scrum-fall-is-the-reality-of-agile); a small measure of agility confined by a traditional waterfall process.

Continuous Delivery

Continuous delivery further extends continuous integration. The output of every code commit is a release candidate that progresses through an automated deployment pipeline to a staging environment, unless it is proven defective. If tests pass, the release candidate is deployable in an automated fashion. Whether or not new functionality is actually deployed comes down to a final business decision. However, it is vital to maintain the ability to deploy at the end of every iteration as opposed to a lengthy waterfall release cycle. This approach considers all of the factors necessary to take an idea from inception to production. The shorter that timeline, the sooner value is realized and further ideas emerge to build upon the previous ones. Companies that operate in this way have a significant advantage and are able to create products that constantly adapt to feedback and user demands.

DevOps

DevOps is a software development and operations culture that has grown in popularity over the recent years. It breaks away from the traditional developer-versus-operation silos, with a focus on communication, collaboration, integration, automation, and measurement of cooperation between all functions required to develop and run applications. The method acknowledges the interdependence of:

- Software development
- Quality assurance and performance tuning
- IT operations
- Administration (SysAdmin, DBAs, etc.)
- Project and release management

DevOps aims to span the full application life cycle to help organizations rapidly produce and operationally maintain performant software products and services.

Traditional silo approaches to IT have led to diametrically opposed objectives that ultimately hinder application quality and speed of delivery. Teams centered around a specialty introduce friction when they inter-operate. An example of friction occurs with change control. Developers achieve success when they innovate and deliver valuable features, so they are constantly pushing for new functionality to be incorporated into a release. Conversely, IT operations achieve success when they minimize churn in favor of reliability, availability, and stability. To mitigate opposing objectives, bureaucratic and time-consuming handoffs occur, resulting in deferred ownership and responsibility. Lack of overall ownership and constant handoffs from one department to the next can prolong a task from minutes or hours to days or weeks.

The DevOps movement has empowered teams to *do what is right* during application development, deployment, and ongoing operations. By eliminating silos and centralizing a collective ownership over the entire development-to-operations life cycle, barriers are quickly broken down in favor of what is best for the application. Shared toolsets and a common language are established around the single goal of developing and supporting software running in production. Applications are not only more robust, they constantly adapt to changing environmental factors. Silos are replaced by collaboration with all members under the same leadership. Burdensome processes are replaced by trust and accountability.

The DevOps culture has produced cross-functional teams centered around a specific business capability. They develop products instead of working on projects. Products, if successful, are long lived. The DevOps team responsible for the development-to-operations lifecycle of a business capability continues to take responsibility for that business capability until it ceases to be in production.

Microservices

Microservices is a term used to describe a software architectural style that has emerged over the last few years. It describes a modular approach to building software in which complex applications are composed of several small, independent processes communicating with each other though explicitly defined boundaries using language-agnostic APIs. These smaller services focus on doing a single task very well. They are highly decoupled and can scale independently.

By adopting a microservices architecture, the nature of what you develop and how you develop it changes. Teams are organized around structuring software in smaller chunks (features, not releases) as separate deployments that can move and scale independently. The act of deploying and the act of scaling can be treated as independent operations, introducing additional speed to scaling a specific component. Backing services are decoupled from application software, allowing applications to be loosely coupled. This ultimately extends the application lifespan as services can be replaced as required.

Business-Capability Teams

By determining the required architecture upfront, organizations can be restructured around business-capability teams that are tasked with delivering the desired architecture. It may be difficult to transition to this in an established enterprise as this approach cuts orthogonally across existing organizational silos. A matrix overlay can help with the transition, but it is worth considering Conway's law:

> "Any organization that designs a system will produce a design whose structure is a copy of the organization's communication structure. "
>
> —Melvyn Conway

Therefore, if you want your architecture to be centered around business capability instead of specialty, you should go *all in* and structure your organization appropriately to match the desired architecture. Once you have adopted this approach, the next step is to define what business-capability teams are needed.

Cloud-Native Applications

An architectural style known as cloud-native applications has been established to describe the design of applications specifically written to run in a cloud environment. These applications avoid some of the anti-patterns that were established in the client-server era, such as writing data to the local file system. Those anti-patterns do not work as well in a cloud environment since, for example, local storage is ephemeral because VMs can move between different hosts. The Twelve Factor App (*http://12factor.net*) explains the 12 principles underpinning cloud-native applications.

Platforms offer a set of contracts to the applications and services that run on them. These contracts ensure that applications are constrained to do the right thing. *Twelve Factor* can be thought of as the contract between an application and a cloud-native platform.

There are benefits to adhering to a contract that constrains things correctly. Twitter is a great example of a constrained platform. You can only write 140 characters, but that constraint becomes an extremely valuable feature of the platform. You can do a lot with 140 characters coupled with the rich features surrounding that contract. Similarly, platform contracts are born out of previous tried and tested constraints; they are enabling and they make doing the right thing easy for developers.

Chapter Summary

This chapter has discussed the following:

- There has been a systemic move to consuming services beyond simply provisioning VMs on demand. Consuming services allows you to focus on building business software against the highest level of abstraction possible.
- For any company to be disruptive through software, it starts with the broad and complete adoptions of IaaS for compute resource to provide on-demand, elastic, and self-service benefits.
- Platforms describe the layer sitting above the IaaS layer, leveraging it directly by providing an abstraction of infrastructure services and a contract for applications and backing services to run and scale.
- Recently there has been a rapid growth in container-based solutions because they offer isolation, resource reuse, and portability.
- Agile development coupled with continuous delivery provides the ability to deploy new functionality at will.
- The DevOps movement has broken down the organizational silos and empowered teams to do what is right during application development, deployment, and ongoing operations.
- Software should be centered around business-capability teams instead of specialty capabilities. This allows for a more modular

approach to building microservices software with decoupled and well defined boundaries. Microservices that have been explicitly designed to thrive in a cloud environment have been termed cloud-native applications.

As a result of these driving forces, cloud-native platforms have been established. The next chapter explores how cloud-native platforms are uniquely positioned to leverage these emerging trends, providing a way to quickly deliver business value.

CHAPTER 3

Cloud-Native Platforms

"Cloud Foundry is so resilient that the reliability of the underlying infrastructure becomes inconsequential."

—Julian Fischer, *anynines*

The previous chapter explored the current technical driving forces impacting software development and delivery. This chapter explores the key concepts that underpin the Cloud Foundry platform and how it is uniquely positioned to leverage the technical driving forces discussed in the previous chapter.

You Need a Cloud-Native Platform, Not a PaaS

Cloud Foundry is a cloud-native platform offering features that can be consumed "as a service." Historically, it has been referred to as a platform as a service (PaaS).

Legacy PaaS

PaaS has been around in various forms for some time; but compared to the IaaS or SaaS layers, PaaS is not well understood because it is an overloaded and ambiguous acronym causing confusion. Everything from configuration-management solutions and middleware-provisioning systems to container-management and orchestration tools have, at some point, all been referred to as a PaaS. Early versions of PaaS struggled to gain broad market adoption because of:

- Limitations around visibility into the platform

- Lack of integration points to extend the platform
- Limited or single language / framework support
- Lock-in concern (due to no open source ecosystem) with a lack of non-public cloud options

The additional challenge with the term PaaS is that the boundaries between SaaS, PaaS, and IaaS are extremely blurred. For example, Amazon now offers a rich set of services natively on its Elastic Compute Cloud (EC2). Does that mean AWS is still just an IaaS, or is it now a PaaS?

The term PaaS should die, if it is not dead already. However, the reality is that the term PaaS is still out there in the marketplace, and its usage may not become obsolete as fast as it should.

Cloud-Native Platforms

Cloud Foundry is an opinionated, structured platform that rectifies the PaaS confusion by imposing a strict contract between:

- The infrastructure layer underpinning it
- The applications and services that it supports

Cloud-native platforms offer a super set of functionality over and above the earlier PaaS offerings. They do far more than provide self-service of resources through abstracting infrastructure. Their inbuilt features, such as resiliency, log aggregation, user management and security, are discussed at length in the next chapter. The key is that cloud-native platforms are designed to do more for you so that you can focus on what is important. Specifically, they are designed to do more (including reliably and predictably running and scaling applications) on top of potentially unreliable cloud-based infrastructure.

Cloud-native platforms are focused on what they enable you to achieve, meaning what is important is not so much what a platform is, or what it does, but rather what it enables you to achieve. What it enables you to achieve is this: it has the potential to make the software build, test, deploy, and scale cycle significantly faster. It removes many of the hurdles involved in deploying software, enabling you to release software at will.

Not all cloud-native platforms are the same. Some are self-built and pieced together from various components; others are black boxed and completely proprietary. The Cloud Foundry cloud-native platform has three defining characteristics: it is structured, opinionated, and open.

The Structured Platform

Within the platform space, two distinct architectural patterns have emerged: structured and unstructured:

- Structured platforms provide built-in capabilities and integration points for key concerns such as enterprise-wide user management, security, and compliance. Everything you need to run your applications should be provided in repeatable way, regardless of what infrastructure you run on. Cloud Foundry is a perfect example of a structured platform.

- Unstructured platforms have the flexibility to define a bespoke solution at a granular level. An example of an unstructured platform would involve a "build your own platform" approach with a mix of cloud-provided services and homegrown tools, assembled for an individual company.

Structured platforms are focused on eliminating the earlier PaaS-related problems mentioned above. For example, Cloud Foundry provides:

- A rich and continuous stream of log information with integration points into application performance management (APM) solutions for visibility into how applications are performing

- A rich set of continually streamed metrics for understanding how the platform itself is operating

- Integration points into existing enterprise technologies (database services, message brokers, LDAP, SAML, etc.)

- Support for numerous languages, frameworks, and services (*polyglot*)

- An open source code base with a large supporting ecosystem, backed by a foundation of over 60 companies and an API not tied to any one vendor

- Support for a number of different deployment options, including public and non-public cloud infrastructure

Structured platforms also focus on simplifying the overall operational model. Rather than integrating, operating, and maintaining numerous individual components, the platform operator just deals with the one platform. Structured platforms remove all the undifferentiated heavy lifting, tasks that must be done—for example, service discovery or application placement—but which are not directly related to revenue-generating software.

While structured platforms are targeted for building new cloud-native applications, they also support legacy application integration where it makes sense to do so, allowing for a broader mix of workloads. Similar to the following argument for opinionated platforms, the structured approach provides a much faster "getting started" experience with a lower overall effort required to operate and maintain the environment.

As a general rule, enterprise businesses gravitate to structured platforms as they offer the "on rails" approach to development and deployment. Some enterprises operate under a perception that their requirements are unique, and therefore, unstructured highly configurable platforms appear appealing. However the reality is that deviation of enterprise requirements, and the need for bespoke solutions is exceptionally low. Unstructured platforms can appeal to startups, as they are typically suited to pure greenfield development with no legacy IT applications or technical debt.

Platform Opinions

When you look at successful software, the greatest and most widely adopted technologies are incredibly opinionated. What this means is that they are built on, and adhere to, a set of well-defined principles employing best practices. They are proven to work in a practical way and reflect how things can and should be done when not constrained by the baggage of technical debt. Opinions produce contracts to ensure applications are constrained to do the right thing.

Like frameworks, which became popular in the early 2000s, platforms are opinionated because they make specific assumptions and optimizations to remove complexity and pain from the user. Frameworks focus on removing implementation pain from developers. This includes removing complex or repetitive tasks that are potentially error prone. The Spring Framework, for example, provides implementations of repetitive "boilerplate code" (code that must exist). Conversely, Java is less opinionated than Spring. If developers do not use opinionated frameworks, they are typically required to develop more code.

Non-opinionated software may support a wider set of use cases through more extensive configuration. They appear attractive at first sight because they can be taken in numerous directions and integrated with several components. You can swap pieces in and out at will and configure and extend it as you wish. However, at scale, these technologies become overly complex and work against you as they move into areas where scaling is limited by implementation complexity or brittle dependencies.

Platforms are opinionated because they make specific assumptions and optimizations to remove complexity and pain from the user. Opinionated platforms are designed to be consistent across environments, with every feature working as designed out of the box. They can still be configurable, and extended, but not to the extent that the nature of the platform changes. Platforms should have opinions on how your software is deployed, run, and scaled, not where an application is deployed; this means that, with respect to infrastructure choice, applications should run anywhere.

The Open Platform

Cloud Foundry is an open platform. It is open on three axes:

1. It allows a choice of IaaS layer to underpin it (AWS, vSphere, etc.).
2. It allows for a number of different developer frameworks, polyglot languages, and application services (Ruby, Go, Spring, etc.).
3. It is open sourced under an Apache 2 license and governed by a multi-organization foundation.

Closed platforms may be proprietary, and often focus on a specific problem. They may only support a single infrastructure, language or use case. Open platforms offer choice where it matters.

Choice of Infrastructure

This first point is crucial: Cloud Foundry is designed to leverage your infrastructure of choice. As such, it has been referred to as the operating system of the cloud (*http://www.jdrosen.net/blog/paas-the-operating-system-of-the-cloud*). It serves as the standard way of leveraging cloud computing resources in order to deploy applications and services.

In the same way that the operating system on your phone, tablet, or laptop abstracts the underlying physical compute resource, Cloud Foundry abstracts the infrastructure's compute resource (specifically virtual storage, networking, RAM, and CPU). The net effect is that Cloud Foundry serves as a standard way to deploy applications and services across different cloud computing resources.

The beauty of this approach is that it does not matter which cloud infrastructure you use, be it AWS, vSphere, OpenStack, Azure, Google, or Photon; Cloud Foundry gives you a platform to deploy against. While IaaS offers many advantages, the underlying platform infrastructure does not have to be cloud based. There is an initiative to support deploying Cloud Foundry directly onto physical servers. However, the principle requirements for self-service, on-demand, and elastic infrastructure still stand.

This infrastructure-agnostic approach provides a uniform API to avoid being locked into a specific infrastructure layer. If you want to have different parts of your business in different places, you are free to do this. This is known as the hybrid cloud approach. With Cloud Foundry, your developers and operators can have very similar user experiences whether on private clouds such as VMware or Openstack, or on public clouds like AWS or Digital Ocean. Applications can be freely moved between environments without complicated refactoring of the application or service layer. This approach is in stark contrast to teams that make direct use of a specific IaaS environments. Directly leveraging IaaS specific APIs requires developer patterns and operations knowledge to be extremely specific to the underlying IaaS technology, frequently resulting in applications tightly coupling to the underlying infrastructure.

Choice of Languages and Services

Developers need a certain level of flexibility and control over how they develop. They need to be allowed to choose the best language and service for the job. If this flexibility is denied them, then innovation can be stifled through conformity. At the same time, however, legitimate requirements exist to ensure that the technology has the appropriate level of governance and support. An employee can build an amazing application, but if it cannot be supported and maintained in production, it is of little use. Therefore, many companies want to standardize at the application layer while allowing a wider array of backing services.

Cloud Foundry can be tailored by a platform operator to offer the appropriate level of choice to the developer. The platform can support a rich set of languages (e.g., Java, Ruby, Go, Python), frameworks (e.g,. Spring, Akka, Play, Rails), and runtime technologies such as Tomcat. In addition, it supports a rich and consistent suite of services and libraries for the developer to leverage.

The Polyglot Dilemma

Some enterprises favor a polyglot approach because they feel that providing developers with choice promotes innovation. Other enterprises favor a streamlined approach of picking a smaller set of languages and services to ease ongoing maintenance and management. The choice is yours; you are free to lock down or open up the language and service choice as you see fit.

What you choose to make available to individual teams and developers is configurable on a per team basis. Configuring an appropriate set of languages and services allows for a diverse set of requirements. Some companies I have worked with offer more than 30 services to their developers. This can make sense in a microservices world where every service is free to implement its own backing store. Other companies may choose to offer only a handful of services, for example, a database such as Postgres, a distributed cache such as Redis, and a message broker such as RabbitMQ.

The Open Source Ecosystem

The middleware estate of well established enterprises has, until recently, included a hefty mix of proprietary middleware such as EJB-based application servers, service oriented architecture (SOA)-based messaging, and commercial monitoring and logging.

Companies embarking on a journey toward a cloud-native platform have, in general, already started a move toward lighter-weight open source components with commercial service and support as required. Cloud Foundry becomes a logical next step in that journey.

Open source is important, not just because it is free, but because anyone can get access to it. Consequently, open source becomes primarily important because it is where ecosystems are being built. Ecosystems have promoted a shift from vendored products controlled by the interest of a single company to open source ecosystems offering a suite of services, battle tested through broad adoption. When an ecosystem is established, it becomes a safe choice for enterprise adoption because you are aligning with a vibrant community pulling in the same direction.

The Cloud Foundry ecosystem is not only backed by open source, it is backed by a foundation. The foundation was born out of a shared belief within its growing community that Cloud Foundry was too important a technology to remain the property of any one vendor. The foundation serves as the home for all the shared intellectual property. It provides the mechanism with which the member organizations and the broader community are able to collaborate and contribute both money and effort. This includes technical contributions to create software from a shared vision to support a common cause.

The foundation currently includes nearly 50 members, and that list continues to expand rapidly. It ensures that the overall direction is not tightly controlled by the interest of one specific vendor but controlled by all the members with the interest of the entire community seen as paramount.

> Products and services that call themselves "Cloud Foundry" are making a commitment to users and to the broader ecosystem that they will offer a common experience across the vendors. For application developers, this means being able to deploy and manage applications in a consistent manner. For platform operations, this means that knowledge and skills are portable across the commercial products. It also means there are clearly defined integration points for the ecosystem to leverage to extend the platform's core functionality.
>
> —Chip Childers, *VP Technology of Cloud Foundry Foundation*

Cloud Foundry Constructs

Cloud Foundry is a cloud-native platform. Cloud-native platforms are essential for adapting to the aforementioned IT trends in Chapter 2. Specifically, the Cloud Foundry platform offers:

- **Services as a higher level of abstraction above infrastructure:** Cloud Foundry provides a self-service mechanism for the on-demand deployment of applications bound to an array of provisioned middleware services. This benefit removes the management overhead of both the middleware and infrastructure layer from the developer, significantly reducing the "development to deployment" time.

- **Containers:** Cloud Foundry supports the use of container images such as Docker as a first-class citizen. It also supports running applications artifacts deployed "as is," containerizing them on the user's behalf. This flexibility allows companies already established with Docker to use their existing assets. Containerizing applications on the user's behalf offers additional productivity and operational benefits because the resulting container image is built from known and vetted platform components, leaving only the application source code to require vulnerability scanning.

- **Agile and automation:** Cloud Foundry can be leveraged as part of a CI/CD pipeline to provision environments and services on demand as the application moves through the pipeline to a production-ready state. This helps satisfy the key Agile requirement of getting code into the hands of end users when required.

- **A cultural shift to DevOps:** Cross-cutting concerns is a well-understood concept by developers. Cloud Foundry is ideally accompanied by a cultural shift to DevOps.

- **Microservices support:** Cloud Foundry supports microservices through providing mechanisms for integrating and coordinating loosely coupled services. In order to realize the benefits of microservices, a platform is required to provide additional supporting capabilities, such as built-in resilience and application authentication.

- **Cloud-native application support:** Cloud Foundry provides a contract for applications to be developed against. This contract makes doing the right thing the easy thing and will result in better application performance, management, and resilience.

Chapter Summary

Cloud Foundry is an opinionated, structured, and open platform.

Opinionated platforms are:

- Built on, and adhere to, a set of well-defined principles employing best practices
- Constrained to do the right thing for your application, based on defined contracts
- Consistent across environments, with every feature working as designed out of the box
- Configurable, and extendable, but not to the extent that the nature of the platform changes

Structured platforms offer:

- A fast "on rails" development and deployment experience
- Lower overall effort required to operate and maintain the environment than unstructured platforms
- Built-in capabilities and integration points for key enterprise concerns such as user management, security, and audit compliance

Cloud Foundry is primarily concerned with how you achieve things and not where you achieve things. The how is key:

- How do you deploy quickly?
- How do you keep applications running?
- How do you provision and bind an application to a service?
- How do you scale?
- How do you stream logs?

The where, as in what type of infrastructure is supporting the platform, or what container engine the application runs in, should be immaterial to the platform and entirely up to you.

This chapter assessed the nature of cloud-native platforms over and above the earlier PaaS offerings. The next chapter focuses on the specific features and benefits of the Cloud Foundry platform.

CHAPTER 4

Do More

"Here is my source code, run it on the cloud for me. I do not care how!"

—Onsi Fakhouri, *VP of Engineering of Pivotal Cloud Foundry*

Platforms abstract the underlying infrastructure and middleware to offer a rich set of capabilities. These capabilities include providing runtime environments and services for running applications. Deploying and configuring middleware consumes time and prolongs release cycles; platforms remove the requirement for this individualized effort.

A primary goal of Cloud Foundry is to enable the development-to-deployment process to be as fast as possible. However, platform capabilities do not stop here. Platforms are intrinsically about doing more. Specifically, platforms take on more of the mandatory *undifferentiated heavy lifting* discussed in Chapter 1. This is beneficial; the less you are required to take on, the higher your velocity will be.

This chapter unpacks Cloud Foundry's capabilities that remove the extraneous and undifferentiated heavy lifting from provisioning infrastructure, runtime environments, applications, and services. The application life cycle may be the same as in the client-server era, but developers can now iterate around that life cycle with velocity, using a self-service model every step of the way.

This chapter explores the following built-in platform capabilities:

- Resiliency and fault tolerance through self-healing and redundancy

- User management

- Security and auditing

- Application life-cycle management, including aggregated streaming of logs and metrics

- Release engineering, including provisioning VMs, containers, middleware, and databases

When there is a technological ecosystem that spends considerable time and effort building these capabilities, it is prudent to leverage them for high-velocity delivery as opposed to spending time and effort building a bespoke, hand-crafted solution.

Resiliency and Fault Tolerance

Cloud Foundry provides built-in resiliency based on control theory. *Control theory* is a branch of engineering and mathematics that uses feedback loops to control and modify the behavior of a dynamic system. Resiliency is about ensuring that the actual system state (the number of running applications, for example) matches the desired state at all times, even in the event of failures; it is an essential but often costly component of business continuity.

Cloud Foundry automates the recovery of failed applications, components, and processes. This *self-healing* removes the recovery burden from the operator, ensuring speed of recovery. Cloud Foundry achieves resiliency and self-healing through:

- Restarting failed system processes

- Recreating missing or unresponsive VMs

- Deployment of new application instances if an application crashes or becomes unresponsive

- Application striping across availability zones to enforce separation of the underlying infrastructure

- Dynamic routing and load balancing

Cloud Foundry deals with application orchestration and placement focused on even distribution across the infrastructure. The user should not have to care about how the underlying infrastructure runs the application beyond having an equal distribution across different resources (known as availability zones). The fact that multiple copies of the application are running with built-in resiliency is what matters.

Cloud Foundry provides dynamic load balancing. Application consumers use a route to access an application; each route is directly bound to one or more applications in Cloud Foundry. When running multiple instances, Cloud Foundry balances the load across the instances, dynamically updating its routing table. Dead application routes are automatically pruned from the routing table with new routes added when they become available.

Without the preceding capabilities, the operations team is required to continually monitor and respond to pager alerts from failed apps and invalid routes. By replacing manual interaction with automated, self-healing software, applications and system components are restored quickly with less risk and downtime. The resiliency concern is satisfied once, for all applications running on the platform, as opposed to developing customized monitoring and restart scripts per application. The platform removes the ongoing cost and associated maintenance of bespoke resiliency solutions.

User Access and Authentication Management

Role-based access defines who can use the platform and how. Cloud Foundry uses role-based access control (RBAC), with each role granting permissions to a specific environment the user is targeting. All collaborators target an environment with their individual user accounts associated with a role that governs what level and type of access the user has within that environment.

Cloud Foundry's User Account and Authentication (UAA) is the central identity-management service for both users and applications. In addition, the UAA's user-identity store can be configured by connecting to external user stores through LDAP or SAML. UAA is based in the latest of security standards like OAuth, OpenID Connect, and SCIM.

Security

Cloud Foundry protects you from security threats by applying security controls and isolating applications and data in the following ways:

- It manages software-release vulnerability using new Cloud Foundry releases, created with timely updates to address code issues.

- It manages OS vulnerability using a new OS created with patches for the latest security fixes.

- It implements role-based access controls, applying and enforcing roles and permissions to ensure that users of the platform can only view and affect the resources they have been granted access to.

- It secures both the code and the configuration of an application within a multitenant environment.

- It deploys each application within its own self-contained and isolated containerized environment.

- It prevents possible denial-of-service attacks through resource starvation.

- It provides an operator audit trail showing all operator actions applied to the platform.

- It provides a user audit trail recording all relevant API invocations of an application.

- It implements network traffic rules (security groups) to prevent system access from and to external networks, production services, and between internal components.

Why is this important? Securing distributed systems is complex. For example, think about these issues:

- How much effort is required to automatically establish and apply network traffic rules to isolate components?

- What policies should be applied to automatically limit resources in order to defend against DoS attacks?

- How do you implement role-based access controls with inbuilt auditing of system access and actions?

- How do you know which components are potentially affected by a specific vulnerability and require patching?

- How do you safely patch the underlying OS without incurring application downtime?

These examples are standard requirements for most systems running in corporate datacenters. The more bespoke engineering you use, the more you need to take on securing and patching that system. Distributed systems increase the security burden because there are more moving parts. Additionally, when it comes to rolling out security patches to update the system, many organizations suffer from configuration drift.

The Challenge of Configuration Drift

Deployment environments (such as staging, QA, and production) are often complex and time-consuming to construct and administer, producing the ongoing challenge of trying to manage configuration drift to maintain consistency between environments and VMs. Reproducible consistency through release engineering tool chains, such as Cloud Foundry's BOSH component, addresses this challenge.

Cloud Foundry manages OS and software-release vulnerability using a new OS and new software releases, created with the required patches for the latest security fixes and code remediation.

Cloud Foundry eases the burden of rolling out these OS and software-release updates. Every component within Cloud Foundry is created with the same OS image. To patch Cloud Foundry, you do not apply the patch to a running OS or component; instead, you redeploy Cloud Foundry with an updated OS or software release. Cloud Foundry's BOSH component redeploys updates component by component to ensure zero-to-minimal downtime. This removes the patching and updating concerns from the operator and provides a safer and more resilient way to update Cloud Foundry while keeping applications running.

In addition to patching, if for any reason a component becomes compromised, it can instantly be recreated using a known and clean software release and OS image, and the compromised component can be removed into a quarantine area for further inspection.

This ability to redeploy Cloud Foundry components at will, from a known, healthy OS image and software release, and with zero-to-minimal downtime, provides an additional level of security and resiliency to the system. Your applications remain available for longer through a simple mechanism for applying updates.

The Application Life Cycle

Typically, in most traditional scenarios, the application developer:

- Develops an application
- Deploys application services
- Deploys an application and connects (binds) it to application services
- Scales an application, both up and down
- Monitors an application
- Upgrades an application

This application life cycle is in play until the application is decommissioned and taken offline. Cloud Foundry simplifies the application life cycle by offering self-service capabilities to the end user. Adopting a self-service approach removes handoffs and potentially lengthy delays between teams. For example, the ability to deploy an application, provision and bind applications to services, scale, monitor, and upgrade are all offered by simple call to the platform.

Traditionally, deploying application code required the provisioning and deploying VMs, operating systems, and middleware to create a development environment for the application to run in. Once that environment was provisioned, it required patching and ongoing maintenance. New environments were then created as the application moved through the deployment pipeline.

With Cloud Foundry, the application or task itself becomes the single unit of deployment. Developers no longer need to concern themselves with which application container to use, which version of Java, and which memory settings or garbage-collection (GC) policy to employ. They just push their application to Cloud Foundry, and it runs. Cloud Foundry removes the cost and complexity of configuring infrastructure and middleware per application. Using a self service model, users can:

- Deploy applications
- Provision and bind additional services, such as messaging engines, caching solutions, and databases
- Scale applications

- Monitor application health and performance
- Update applications
- Delete applications

Removing the infrastructure, OS, and middleware configuration concerns from developers allows them to focus their whole effort on the application instead of deploying and configuring the supporting technologies. This keeps the development focus where it needs to be, on the business logic that generates revenue.

Aggregated Streaming of Logs and Metrics

Cloud Foundry provides insight into both the application and the underlying platform through aggregated logging and metrics. The logging and metrics system within Cloud Foundry is the inner voice of the system, telling the operator and developer what is happening. It is used to manage the performance, health, and scale of running applications and the platform itself.

Logs provide visibility into the behavior of running applications and system components, while metrics provide visibility into the health of components running the application. Operators can use metrics information to monitor an instance of Cloud Foundry.

Insights are obtained through storing and analyzing a continuous stream of aggregated, time-ordered events from the output streams of all running processes and backing services. The benefits of aggregated log, metric, and event streaming include the following:

- Logs are streamed to a single endpoint.
- Streamed logs provide timestamped outputs per application.
- Both application logs and system-component logs are aggregated, simplifying their digestion.

- A metrics collector gathers and streams metrics from the system components.

- Operators can use metrics information to monitor an instance of Cloud Foundry.

- Logs can be viewed from the command line or drained into a log management service such as an ELK stack or Splunk.

- Events show specific events like an application being started or stopped. Viewing events is useful when you are debugging problems by identifying crash information, such as a memory limit being exceeded.

The cost of implementing an aggregated log and metrics-streaming solution involves bespoke engineering to orchestrate and aggregate the streaming of both syslog and application logs from every component within a distributed system into a central server. Using a platform removes the ongoing cost and associated maintenance of bespoke logging solutions.

Release Engineering through BOSH

IT operations are tasked with achieving operational stability. Historically, operational stability was achieved by reducing risk through limiting change. Limiting change is in direct conflict to shipping smaller features frequently. In order to manage risks involved in frequent software releases, release-engineering tool chains are used. Release engineering is the part of the operations team typically concerned with turning source code into finished software components or products through the following steps:

- Compilation
- Versioning
- Assembly/packaging
- Deploying

Automating release-engineering concerns through a tool chain reduces risk, allowing for faster deployments with little to no human interaction.

Release-engineering tool chains are essential because they provide consistent repeatability. Source code, third-party components, data, and deployment environments of a software system are integrated and deployed in a repeatable and consistent fashion, with a historical view to track all changes made to the deployed system. This provides the ability to audit and identify all components that make up a particular release. Security teams can easily track contents of a particular release and recreate it at will if the need arises. *Consistent repeatability de-risks software releases.*

Cloud Foundry leverages a release-engineering tool chain known as BOSH. BOSH is a recursive acronym for BOSH Outer Shell. The outer shell refers to BOSH being a release tool chain that unifies release-engineering, deployment and life-cycle management of cloud-based software. BOSH is designed for large distributed systems such as Cloud Foundry but can equally be used to deploy smaller individual components such as etcd (*https://github.com/ coreos/etcd*) or redis (*http://redis.io/*).

Rather than leveraging a bespoke integration of a variety of tools and techniques that provide solutions to individual parts of the release engineering goal, BOSH is designed to be a single tool covering the entire set of requirements of release engineering. BOSH enables software deployments to be:

- Automated
- Reproducible
- Scalable
- Monitored with self-healing failure recovery
- Updatable with zero-to-minimal downtime

BOSH translates intent into action via repeatability by always ensuring that every provisioned release is identical and repeatable. This removes the challenge of configuration drift.

BOSH configures infrastructure through code. By design, BOSH tries to abstract away the differences between infrastructure platforms (IaaS or physical servers) into a generalized, cross-platform description of your deployment. This provides the benefit of being infrastructure agnostic (as far as possible).

BOSH performs monitoring, failure recovery, and software updates with zero-to-minimal downtime. Without such a release-engineering tool chain, all these concerns remain the responsibility of the operations team. A lack of automation exposes the developer to unnecessary risk.

Deploying and Scaling

Deploying and scaling applications are completely independent operations. This provides the flexibility to scale at will, without the cost of having to redeploy the application every time. Through commercial products such as Pivotal Cloud Foundry, auto-scaling policies can also be set up for dynamic scaling of applications when they hit certain configurable thresholds.

A Marketplace of On-Demand Services

Applications often require additional services. For example, they may require a persistent datastore for storing information or a message broker for communicating with other applications. Each environment within Cloud Foundry has the concept of a marketplace. A marketplace lists the services that have been made available to that specific environment by the platform operator. A service can offer different service plans to provide varying levels of resources or features for the same service. An example of service plans is a database service offering small, medium, or large plans with differing levels of concurrent connections and storage sizes. Service instances can be provisioned on demand by a user. The provisioned service provides a unique set of credentials that can be used to bind and connect an application to the service.

Chapter Summary

Cloud Foundry does more on your behalf with the use of all its features and the BOSH release engineering tool chain.

Cloud Foundry provides:

- Built-in resiliency through automated recovery and self-healing of failed applications, components, and processes
- Built-in resiliency through striping applications across different resources
- Authentication and authorization for both users and applications, with the addition of role-based access control for users
- Inbuilt security

- The ability to update the platform with zero-downtime rolling upgrades across the system
- Applications with the ability to connect to an infinite array of services via both platform-managed service brokers and services running in the existing IT infrastructure
- Built-in management and operation services for your application, such as metrics and log aggregation, monitoring, auto-scaling, and performance management

CHAPTER 5

Breaking Down Silos

"Blame the process, not the people."

—W. Edwards Deming

In Chapter 1, I made the argument that technology alone has never been enough. Companies need to fundamentally change the way they build and deploy software. This chapter explores the recommended changes and practical considerations that pave the way for the successful adoption of Cloud Foundry

Embracing Cloud Foundry

Organizations cannot simply drop Cloud Foundry into a data center and expect overnight success if nothing else changes. *Process, cultural,* and *organizational* change must accompany the technical changes. The extent of the change, for many established businesses, will require a shift in how they think about and approach development and IT operations.

One strategic benefit is that companies can actually use Cloud Foundry to drive and shape the required changes. Cloud Foundry can become a powerful and compelling point of leverage for drawing people into the cultural shift. Change for most people and most companies is still a significant undertaking, however much they are drawn to it.

I have observed two approaches to the enterprise adoption of Cloud Foundry:

1. Decentralized deployments
2. A shared centralized deployment

There are advantages and pitfalls to both approaches.

Decentralized Deployments

Decentralized deployments allow each individual business capability team to leverage its own dedicated platform.

One benefit of this approach is that individual teams can move at their own pace, configuring a dedicated Cloud Foundry platform and related services to suit their requirements; there is no need to try to change an entire company in one go. The wave of Cloud Foundry adoption can be incremental, established on a team-by-team basis.

A requirement for this approach is that each business capability team has control and expertise over the underlying infrastructure and resources; the lack of prevalence of required skills within a company can be a hurdle to overcome with this approach. The risk of platform *snowflakes* (because each platform is operated by different teams) is often a challenge. Operational efficiencies and elimination of platform *configuration drift* can be more easily achieved by a centralized approach.

Shared Centralized Deployment

Companies who do not want to deploy an instance of Cloud Foundry per business capability team tend to adopt a centralized approach via the formation of a platform-operations team.

The Platform Operations Team

Establishing a dedicated team with the specific business-capability focus of deploying and running a cloud-native platform is a key requirement for successfully adopting and running a centralized Cloud Foundry environment.

The platform operations team's overall responsibility is deploying and operating the self-service platform that other business-capability teams can then leverage.

Typical roles required for this team include:

- Networking administrator
- Storage administrator
- System administrator
- IaaS administrator
- Software developer/application architect
- Security auditor
- QA/performance tester
- Release management
- Project management

These are not necessarily nine exclusive roles; individuals may combine a number of the preceding capabilities. For example, an IaaS administrator may also have storage experience. Most of these roles —networking and security, for example—are more relevant at the beginning when setting up the platform and operational processes. It is often sufficient just to maintain a regular point of contact for ongoing expertise in these areas.

If Cloud Foundry is deployed on premises as opposed to on hosted virtual infrastructure such as AWS, then the platform-operations team will need to work closely with teams responsible for the physical infrastructure in the data centers. This is both to help facilitate capacity planning and because an understanding and appreciation of the hardware capabilities underpinning the IaaS layer is required to ensure a sufficient level of availability.

There is a software development role in the mix because it is necessary to define and understand the application requirements and best practices based on *Twelve Factor* applications. Additionally, the platform-operations team needs to appreciate the application services required to support cloud-native apps. Developers often have specific requirements for choosing a particular technology appropriate for their application. This need can be magnified in a world of microservices where each service should be free to leverage an appropriate backing technology. The platform-operations team should work directly with other business-capability teams to ensure that they offer a rich and defined portfolio of platform services. These services can be hosted directly on the platform where it makes sense to do so, instead of being operated and connected adjacent to the platform.

Cloud Foundry allows the platform operator to define *orgs*, which notionally embody a business unit, and *spaces*, which notionally embody the area where a team within a business unit would deploy their software. These are logical constructs, and an individual developer can belong to multiple orgs and spaces and have different authorities assigned accordingly. Because orgs and spaces are logical separations, you are free to structure them as you see fit. However, encapsulating business units comprised of smaller teams, who are centered on specific business capabilities, provides a good abstraction for org and space boundaries.

The question of who defines the logical separations within Cloud Foundry often comes up. The platform-operations team often works with the various business-capability teams to define a structure that works for the wider organization.

The platform-operations team is the primary point of contact for any operational issues or feature requests for the Cloud Foundry platform and related services. There needs to be a cultural change to move away from ticket-based systems to presenting an API contract for the platform services. This allows business-capability teams to adopt the approach of building automated release pipelines that can provision environments and services on demand. This ability supports the endeavor for continuous delivery.

Changing the Culture

As discussed at length in Chapter 2, in order to truly ship with velocity you need to embrace the myriad technical forces impacting software development.

Regardless of the deployment approach (centralized or decentralized platforms), a cultural shift toward DevOps and agility through XP is required.

- DevOps promotes the breakdown of *silos of specialty* into *business capability teams*. As discussed in "DevOps" on page 16, each individual business capability team has collective ownership over the entire development-to-operations life cycle of its software.

- The underlying values of XP are communication, simplicity, feedback, courage, and respect. XP promotes changing team dynamics to establish a culture of high trust coupled with low (unrestrictive) process, with individual freedom and responsibility for successes and failures.

Embracing Trust and Accountability

If you want to move quickly, then you have to trust your team to be accountable and do the right thing. Lack of trust often stifles speed and innovation because imposed processes remove ownership and introduce handoffs and delays. Information and collaboration must flow freely, at least internally, to enable speed.

Regardless of the approach to adopting Cloud Foundry, a cultural shift to DevOps and XP will maximize its benefits. Consider the following scenario:

A company may ultimately desire dedicated Cloud Foundry deployment per business capability team. However, if you begin by building a single centralized Cloud Foundry, this is not anti-DevOps if every business unit has full rights to the platform.

A centralized deployment works if representatives from every line of business are communicating with each other both effectively and respectfully, providing constant feedback and continuous process improvements. *Collective platform ownership* established by a platform-operations team is a reasonable starting point. When one team has specific requirements that are in direct conflict with another team's, they are free to deploy their own Cloud Foundry while maintaining autonomy so that all teams can continue to ship with velocity.

The anti-pattern to avoid is allowing a single platform-operations team to become the new "infrastructure" team that locks the business capability teams out. This approach is anti-DevOps as you have not changed the pattern of communication or flattened the silos. While developers can leverage the platform contract, they have no direct control or autonomy over the platform, so they are locked out from key capabilities, like adding new services. In short, you must avoid recreating your old environment with a new tool. Ensuring full rights to the platform by adding representatives from each business capability team to the platform-operations team can maintain the desired DevOps and agile culture.

The Platform Champion

For many large and well-established enterprises, it can be extremely hard to break through emergent behaviors that hinder deployment of software. Emergent behavior occurs as several independent business functions interoperate, forming a collective set of complex interactions and behaviors. Emergent behavior does not arise by deliberate design, but once bad emergent behavior is established, it requires conscious effort and collective agreement to change it.

Change to emergent behavior is often pioneered by a platform champion. The essence of this role is to bring about cultural shifts and widespread platform adoption throughout the different application/business teams. The role should be taken up by someone senior enough to have influence, either directly or indirectly, vertically up to the CTO/CIO level and horizontally across the individual lines of business.

Consider the consequences of not filling this role. Cloud Foundry can be established by a single team, often the operations team, with a passion for doing things differently. However, if there is no adoption across the lines of business, the full value of the platform may not be realized. To quote one company I have recently been working with:

> "You can be surrounded by all the best-of-breed technology you desire, but if you don't have a chance to apply it to something, what's the point?"

This role is not unique to a centralized deployment model. The platform champion should be fundamental in establishing the required cultural shift to DevOps and XP. They should passionately protect the right culture without letting the old culture creep back in.

Chapter Summary

DevOps, agile, XP, continuous delivery, cloud-native platforms, and microservices have emerged from the same set of principles. They are focused on enabling organizations to ship software with velocity. And they are dynamic and evolving as these communities cooperate and drive innovation forward.

This chapter explored the considerations required to adopt Cloud Foundry in an established enterprise. These include the removal of silos and establishing the right culture and people, either in decentralized teams or in a single centralized platform-operations team, as well as appointing someone within the organization who will champion change.

The effect of achieving *process*, *organization*, and *culture* change is that business can move at a phenomenal pace. Moving quickly allows developers to reflect on and respond to consumer feedback, which ultimately produces software that aligns tightly with user expectations.

CHAPTER 6

Summary

"We excel at focusing on the things that only we can do, which means leaving certain things to others who excel at what THEY do; this is why we work with Cloud Foundry."

—Harel Kodesh, *CTO of GE Digital*

This book has explored a number of technical driving forces impacting software development and delivery. These driving forces are far more than hype; they provide intrinsic value. To recap:

- Agile is not just the adoption of stories and scrums. It involves a completely different approach from the traditional waterfall development model, with the most critical element being rapid feedback from end users.

- Continuous delivery is not about automation for the sake of reducing cost. It is about ensuring that repeatable, tested, and integrated releases can be placed in the hands of the consumer when required, rather than waiting for an annual release cycle.

- Microservices are not merely about delivering smaller services. They are about faster development of more modular applications with the freedom to be decoupled in development and connected in deployment.

- Cloud-native applications do not simply mean applications running on an IaaS. They are applications designed to thrive and move at will in an ephemeral and highly distributed environment.

If the preceding trends are actively contrasted with traditional enterprise IT, one thing becomes clear. Most teams are full of very talented individuals who, collectively, are a long way from moving at the required pace of change. Companies that cannot deliver software at the required cadence need to fundamentally change the way they build and deploy software in order to succeed in the hugely competitive markets that exist today. These companies need to become cloud native.

Becoming Cloud Native

We have discussed becoming *cloud native* as an imperative for delivering applications with velocity. Becoming cloud native involves adopting three key elements:

- Self-service, on-demand, and elastic infrastructure
- Cloud-native platforms
- Cloud-native / Twelve Factor applications

Adopting these three elements provides the capabilities required for:

- Repeatedly delivering software into production with velocity
- Establishing a timely development-feedback cycle

Cloud-native platforms have become essential for adapting to the aforementioned IT trends. They are focused on making the software build, test, deploy, and scale cycle significantly faster. They achieve this by removing many of the hurdles involved in deploying software, enabling you to release software at will. In short, Cloud Foundry does more on your behalf, purposefully allowing enterprises to refocus engineering effort back into the business. This is beneficial; the less you are required to do, the higher your velocity will be.

Why Cloud Foundry?

Cloud Foundry is an opinionated, structured cloud-native platform that imposes a strict contract between the infrastructure layer underpinning it and the applications and services that it supports. This allows for cloud-native applications to be run predictably and reliably across different infrastructures.

Cloud Foundry is an open platform, allowing for a choice of underlying infrastructure, polyglot developer languages and frameworks, and a rich array of application services. In addition, Cloud Foundry is open sourced and governed by a multi-organization foundation. The diversity, strength, and value of this community should not be underestimated. It is a powerful thing when different technology companies, industries, and lines of business collaborate with such strong cohesion and momentum.

Enabling the Fundamental Shift

Business value is no longer sustainable by maintaining a process to support an established competitive advantage. Markets and business climates are changing too rapidly for this approach to be sustainable. Specifically, established markets are being repeatedly disrupted by software. Technology is constantly evolving, and businesses are under relentless pressure to adopt the myriad of technical driving forces impacting software development and delivery.

These driving forces are all focused on enabling organizations to ship software with velocity; velocity is paramount to establishing a competitive advantage. Companies need to adapt to these driving forces—constantly evaluating, adopting, and incorporating the necessary technologies, development methodologies, and architectural styles—in order to remain competitive.

Ongoing competitive advantage is established through delivering software repeatedly, with velocity, through iterative development cycles of short duration, resulting in a constant feedback loop from end users.

Technology alone, however, has never been enough. Companies need to fundamentally change the way they build and deploy software. Velocity is achieved by making the necessary technical changes along with changes to established process, organization, and culture. The effect of achieving this change is that business can move at a phenomenal pace. Moving at pace enables companies to react to shifting demand and focus on the key areas receiving the most customer traction. Ultimately, it produces software that aligns tightly with user expectations. This is your new competitive advantage.

Cloud Foundry, with the backing of a vibrant open source community and an established foundation nearing 60 companies, is arguably one of the most important open source projects in existence today.

For those companies desiring to achieve velocity and establish a development-feedback cycle—and for those companies challenged with responding to the technical driving forces relentlessly shaping today's marketplaces—Cloud Foundry, as an established cloud-native platform, provides the most compelling way to enable the fundamental shift in the way we build and deploy software.

About the Author

With a deep passion for bridging enterprise operations and development, **Duncan Winn** has been working with Cloud Foundry since 2012. He works with numerous companies to help them establish hardened production-ready Cloud Foundry environments and related services. Prior to moving to the US, he was the EMEA Cloud Foundry Developer Advocate for Pivotal. He organized the London Cloud Foundry Meetup and ran Pivotal's UK Field Engineering team. He is very active in the Cloud Foundry community and runs the blog *thisweekincf.com*.

About the Author